650 | Love and Marriage

Edited by Edward McCann

650 | WHERE WRITERS READ

Founder / Editor • Edward McCann
Executive Producer • Richard Kollath
Literary Ombudsman / Senior Editor • Steven Lewis
Director of Operations • Jane Kaupp
Design Director • Diane Fokas
Social Media Strategist • Shayna Miller
Director of Photography • Kevin O'Connor
Chief Audio Engineer • Jesse Chason
Videography / Photography • Sara Caldwell
Copy Editor • Shelley Sadler Kenney
Technical Advisor • Conrad Trautmann
Technical Advisor • Stephen Kaupp

Production Assistants
Robert Dennison, Lynn Dennison, Mackenzie Meeks,
Jackie Mercurio, Brian Reagher, and Isabella Fokas

Advisory Committee
Rachel Aydt, Laura Shaine Cunningham, Angela Davis-Gardner,
Karen Dukess, Joseph Goodrich, David Masello, Honor Molloy,
Irene O'Garden, John Pielmeier, Gretchen Reed, James Russek,
Angela Derecas Taylor and Julie Trelstad

"Love doesn't just sit there, like a stone, it has to be made, like bread; remade all the time, made new."
—*Ursula Le Guin*

ABOUT 650

Love is all you need. Love is like oxygen. Love will keep us together. Like corny song lyrics, love is all around, and sometimes we're lucky enough to share some, to give some, to receive some. But love is different from marriage, and, while they may go together like ... well, like a horse and carriage, these are two very different things that also exist quite independent from each other—as you will read in the pages that follow.

650 is a celebration of writing and the spoken word, a literary forum for personal stories performed five minutes—and 650 words—at a time. Our events at theaters, colleges, and libraries around the country are organized around single, broad topics that invite a range of expression, and recorded performances are added to a digital archive of writers reading their work aloud. The writers and their work receive additional exposure through podcasts, broadcasts, our YouTube channel, and in these printed volumes. The volume you hold in your hands is a collection of stories featured at our first event at Sarah Lawrence College in Westchester County, New York.

650 features graduate students and grandparents, first-timers and best-selling writers. It's all about the writing, with an emphasis on craft. It's about the choice of one word over another, about the shape of sentences and paragraphs, the arc of a narrative, the poetry of a unique literary voice. If you love language and enjoy a good story, you've come to the right place. To submit your work or attend our shows, visit our website or Facebook page, and join our mailing list.

Please tell your friends about 650, and spread the word about the spoken word.

Ed McCann

Edward McCann, Founder / Editor

READ650.COM
FACEBOOK.COM/READ650

CONTENTS

650 | Love and Marriage

Edited by Edward McCann

MARGARITA MEYENDORFF

Margarita Meyendorff (Mourka) is the author of the memoir *DP: Displaced Person.* The daughter of a Russian baron, she was born displaced, far from the opulence of Imperial Russia that was her birthright. A series of wars destroyed this privileged existence, and Margarita's life became a series of extraordinary moves. She has performed as an actress, dancer, musician, and storyteller at venues throughout the United States and in Europe.

NORTH CAPE MAY

Margarita Meyendorff

I noticed Miky standing at the express counter at the Grand Union in Kingston, New York. He was very handsome. I knew he was Hungarian because we had previously met through my Bulgarian-then boyfriend. Miky and I spoke. I couldn't help but notice his low sexy baritone voice. I told Miky that I would be singing with a Russian ensemble and that I hoped he'd attend the show. He gave me his phone number. Who could know that this little exchange would lead to a "grand union" — a blissful marriage of nineteen years?

In 1997 when our romance began, we were broke. I was out of work and launching my one-woman show in NYC and Miky worked three jobs — an engineer for Ulster County, a taxi driver for Kingston Cabs, and a vegetable cutter for a Chinese restaurant. He was putting his daughter and son through Bard College and was in debt up to his ears.

That July, Miky and I decided to go camping in North Cape May, New Jersey — an inexpensive way to enjoy the sandy beaches and warm waters of the Jersey shore. We invested in a spacious tent

1

that could sleep four—we would have none of the tiny claustrophobic tents. We bought a queen-sized air mattress and a pump to make it expand to a luxurious-feeling bed. We brought food, pans and utensils to cook outdoors, wood for the fire and several bottles of wine. We packed, hung the bicycles on the bike rack and set off for the five-hour trip to Cold Spring Campground.

It was hot, well over ninety degrees. We arrived at the campsite early enough to bike to the closest beach. A narrow path through thick woods hanging with wild roses and honeysuckle led us to Higbee Beach on the Delaware Bay. To our surprise, we were greeted by a massive Voodoo sign criss-crossed on two timbers and a group of suntanned, smiling, naked people who welcomed us to the nude beach and encouraged us to take off our clothes—which we did. So much for Victorian Cape May and the conservative state of New Jersey. We swam naked in the warm, murky waters of the bay, frolicked on the beach and watched as the Cape May-Lewes Ferry headed out toward Delaware and disappeared in the mist.

The sun was setting when we got dressed and biked to our campsite. We opened up a bottle of wine as we pitched the tent, inflated the mattress and started the fire to make dinner. We opened up the second bottle of wine as I scrubbed the potatoes, wrapped them in tin foil and threw them onto the coals. I made salad and Miky prepared the chicken. He placed the chicken into the frying pan and let it sizzle as we gobbled up the salad. We were famished ... and not a little tipsy from the wine.

We heard a kind of a popping squeaky sound coming from the

frying pan as bubbles started to form around the pieces of chicken. In our inebriated state, we thought we were hallucinating as the bubbles grew bigger and bigger and the chicken seemed to come to life as it rose as if by magic from the pan. But then we noticed that the chicken had an odd scent, similar to soap.

It *was* soap.

I had mistaken the dish soap for olive oil when I started to fry the chicken. Without hesitation, Miky lifted the chicken out of the frying pan, placed it into a sieve, then washed it under the faucet; we then finished frying it in olive oil. A bit fragrant but otherwise delicious! Throughout the dinner we laughed, and we laughed as we stumbled into our bed. The next morning, we were still laughing as we passed gas that was pungent with perfumed detergent. It didn't matter. We felt effervescent in every sense. We were in love. Everything was possible.

JOSEPH BURGO

Joseph Burgo is a clinical psychologist in private practice and the author of both self-help books and novels. His essays have appeared in *The New York Times*, *The Atlantic*, and other major publications; a recognized expert on narcissism, he is frequently quoted in *USA Today*, *Glamour*, the *Huffington Post* and other major news outlets. His newest book, *Shame*, was published in fall 2018 by St. Martin's Press. He writes a blog on the topic of shame and discusses personality development issues on his website, *After Psychotherapy*.

KITTY AND VRONSKY AT THE BALL

Joseph Burgo

In the declining years of my first marriage, I confided to a friend that if my wife and I were to divorce, I'd never remarry. My reason: I couldn't bear ever again to feel that I was such a deep disappointment to another human being. I saw myself as a failure; I felt certain that my wife viewed me as a failed husband. I vowed never to grant another person the power to burden me with so much shame.

In the two decades since, I've come to think of shame as a kind of unrequited love, an insight that struck me one night during a bout of insomnia when I was reading Anna Karenina and came upon the following passage: "Kitty and Vronsky are dancing together at a ball. Kitty believes herself to be in love with Vronsky and, until this moment, has believed the feeling to be reciprocated.

"Kitty looked into his face, which was so close to her own, and long afterwards—for several years after—that look, full of love, to which he made no response, cut her to the heart with an agony of shame."

When I first read that passage, I felt startled, and unprepared for the sentence to end in the word shame. But the more I've thought about it, both with my psychotherapy clients and in my personal life, I've come to understand that to love and find oneself unloved in return is the very essence of shame. To gaze with love as Kitty does and to be met with indifference can rob us, at least for a time, of our sense of self-worth.

By contrast, to love someone and feel loved by that very person—well, nothing makes us feel better—about being alive and about being who we are. It's the way we're supposed to begin life, adored by parents who make us feel beautiful and worthy. I did not begin life that way. I spent my late teens and early twenties trying to experience mutual joy and love for the first time, so desperate for it that I'd rush into bed or fall headlong in love with anyone who made me feel beautiful or wanted. Lots of promiscuous sex, lots of disillusionment, lots of shame about my disastrous choices. But when I finally married, I thought, at long last, I'd chosen well.

Sometimes it feels as if it's been a lifetime of shame.

And yet, here I am, recently married to my partner of fourteen years and writing a book that's all about shame. About shame but also about joy. In spite of what I told my friend two decades ago, I find that I'm an optimist after all when it comes to love. For people like me who've struggled with shame throughout their lives, finding mutual joy and love with another person can be wonderfully healing. It's not the same as having started out in life with an adored mother who adored you in return, but it goes a long way toward healing the damage.

After fourteen years together, I sometimes awaken in the middle of the night, and the sight of his sleeping body next to mine can still make me smile. He is beautiful to me. At the end of the work day when I come upstairs from my office—when he turns in his chair to greet me and I can see on his face that he's been eagerly awaiting me—in addition to all the other emotions he inspires in me, I also feel good about myself.

And there's no shame in that.

MARLENA MADURO BARAF

Marlena Maduro Baraf, born and raised in Panama, now lives and works in New York. She studied at Occidental College in Los Angeles and Parsons School of Design in New York, where she is principal at an interior design firm. Marlena also worked as Editor with the McGraw-Hill Book Company and has been active in the Sarah Lawrence College writing community. Her work has appeared in the *Westchester Review, Blue Lyra Review, Lumina Journal*, and other publications. She blogs the Soy/Somos series with *Latino Voices* at the *Huffington Post,* deeply committed to creating a real-life collage of Latinos in the US.

MY FIRST AMERICAN DATE

Marlena Maduro Baraf

I was an immigrant from a small banana republic, eleven months in New York City. Long enough to grow weary of gringos crying triumphantly, "Ah yes! The Panama Canal!" "Where exactly is Panama?"

I shared a crypt-like studio on Madison and 62nd with a view of a wall. I'd found work with an English as a Second Language publisher and was taking a drawing class at night. At eleven months plus ten days, a co-worker in my office said, "I know a guy who would really like you. American. His name's Daniel; born in Brooklyn. Studied in Chile for six months."

To Daniel he said, "She's got big tits."

I wore my red-knit dress. It had a peek-a-boo keyhole above the chest.

Daniel fetched me at my apartment with a view of a wall, took me to an Irish Pub. I noticed his hands. They curved gently toward his chest as he bantered with the proprietor of the pub. "Bring us your old crackers and cheese, Frank. And a whiskey sour for the lady."

Piano player's hands, I thought. I pulled out the drawing book that I carried in my purse. Daniel's tapered fingers landed on the gouged, dark wood table in the dimly lit room. He didn't seem to mind my light sketching. It was a very small notebook.

As I drew, Daniel went on and on about Chile. "The situation was confusing in Santiago in 1961. There was so much poverty. There were seven political parties and people could not agree on the shape of an egg."

He was all head. His brain had to be huge!

I couldn't help staring at his mouth. His moving mouth. His voice was deep and melodious. His puffy lips not like my own tapering bow. I looked into his green eyes as I sized him up with my amber pencil. Light brown curls. Ears close to his skull. Small nose. Almost...handsome.

"I had never been abroad," he said. "At the stadium for a game of futbol, I saw that Chilenos ate peanuts. Unshelled peanuts. Same as at Ebbets Field in Brooklyn. This shocked me."

I asked if Brooklyn was part of New York.

Daniel said he'd traveled alone during his senior year at Princeton with a theme of his own choosing: to study the effects of the Cuban revolution on the political life in Chile. An impossibly huge topic. He'd met Senador Allende, he said. He'd found a room at the university and read six newspapers every day. Almost no one with whom to speak in English. They pointed at him and laughed at his trench coat. "Gringo, we don't wear raincoats here. Ja ja ja."

I'd ask a question or two. His gaze would make a flash landing on my chest.

I continued to draw in my very small notebook as Daniel spoke about beisbol, about "los lanzadores" that he saw in Panama where he'd stopped for two days on his open airline ticket on Panagra while returning to New York from Chile. He made faces when he spoke in Spanish, lengthening syllables with a mock José Jiménez accent. I laughed.

He seemed unaware of my moving pencil. He said I was "eclectic." "It's my best compliment," he assured me. "You don't fit any pattern. You have many interests." (Though I hadn't said much.)

We heard the cry behind us. "Fire!" A fire in the kitchen sent the patrons scrambling out of the pub onto the streets of the Village. Daniel quickly grabbed his trench coat with multiple buttons and belts and laid it on my shoulders. He glanced at the peek-a-boo keyhole. His fingers pressed softly on my neck.

So I wonder if you've guessed it. We were married a year later.

KATHY CURTO

Kathy Curto teaches at The Writing Institute at Sarah Lawrence College, Montclair State University, and across the metropolitan area serving writers of all ages. Her work has been published in the anthology, *Listen to Your Mother: What She Said Then, What We're Saying Now,* and in publications including *Barrelhouse, Drift, Talking Writing, Junk, The Inquisitive Eater, the Asbury Park Press, Italian Americana, VIA-Voices in Italian Americana* and *Lumina Journal.* In 2006, she was awarded the Kathryn Gurfein Writing Fellowship at Sarah Lawrence College and also served as a 2015 to 2016 engaged teaching fellow at Montclair State. Kathy lives in Cold Spring, New York with her husband and their four children.

WHAT HE KNEW

Kathy Curto

The kids were one, three, five and six. We had no business going away with them in tow, but we were trying to stay sane and in love so we went anyway. I wanted no laundry and a meal I didn't cook. He wanted a break from work. And the kids wanted to take turns pushing a hotel elevator button. I booked a place, Mountaintop Lodge, ninety minutes away with a room that fit us all. I didn't ask about dress codes. I didn't ask about dinner seating. I didn't ask about what I now know are defined as additional charges.

In the lobby we were greeted with an onslaught of pastel sweater sets and loafers. Lots and lots of loafers. My faded jean jacket was clearly the wrong call. All eyes were on the jacket and my son, Sam. His Buzz Lightyear pajamas smelled sour and Buzz's face was stained with a blob of Yoo-hoo. Hushed remarks about the girls, too, were likely--with their uneven ponytails and the stick-on fake fingernail tips in neon colors.

I thought this was a lodge. To me, lodge meant jeans, hot dogs and s'mores. Not pressed khakis, beef Wellington and petits fours. Or afternoon tea.

"One or two keys, sir?" asked Audrey, the Reservation Specialist to my husband, Peppe.

"Two's good," he answered and signed the card that allowed us to charge our every move. Because, in addition to looking nothing like a lodge, it also didn't match my idea of what a lodge costs. There would be no cherries in the Shirley Temples for us.

We got through dinner probably because we employed *Operation If You Behave* as a means of survival. The kids wanted to play after so we rolled out our favorite strategy: leverage.

Earlier Audrey told us all about the "magnificent" game room. "And for your little princesses we have "spectacular" costumes!" Audrey winked, too, but looked away when she noticed two of our three princesses picking their noses.

So after dinner we went to the game room where they played dress-up and Cinderella pinball. There was even a make-your-own cotton candy machine, which is just what their already inappropriate outfits didn't need. We were done.

But as we left we noticed a dim backroom. Inside, a pool table. "When was the last time you played pool?" Peppe asked.

"College, I think," I said, realizing what that meant. We never played pool together.

"How about one game?" he nudged.

The kids were tired and sticky. But some higher power

pulled them onto the fancy leather couch next to the pool table. They curled up into one another and squealed.

"No, let me watch you," I said and sat on a stool in the corner next to the sticks and chalk and ball racks. I had forgotten something about myself but when he reached for the cue stick, I was reminded.

There's a slow, smooth, deliberate manner of leaning that must happen to play pool well. He knew about that.

Then there are the ways hands and fingers and legs must work to play the game. Knew that, too.

There are the sounds. The cracks and echoes that arouse, thrill, and startle. The breaks, stunts, and tricks. There's the jukebox and there's Muddy Waters.

There are the eyes. How they watch, deepen and consider. And the way they shift up, just before the shot, maybe to see who's watching.

He looked up at me and let his cue slide forward. My eyes dwelled on his for a handful of seconds and then an epiphany: I may not have gotten off the stool but we were both playing in this game.

Still.

I gazed from him to the kids who were tangled up and almost asleep on Mountaintop's fancy leather couch.

I watched him some more.

And there, in my faded jean jacket, I was shaken and stirred.

HONOR FINNEGAN

Honor Finnegan has been singing and performing since she was a child. She was in the first national tour of *Annie,* performed at the Improv Olympic, Chicago's premiere venue for improvisational comedy, and won accolades for songwriting and performing folk music. After a dramatic experience in 2016 involving a flash flood in Texas, Honor began writing (mostly) first person essays, and participating in slams at *The Moth.* She is also a preschool educator/ special educator, a Heartfulness Meditation trainer, and mother to one adult son. She currently resides in Dubai, where she teaches Pre-K at the Bank Street-affiliated Clarion School.

MONEY

Honor Finnegan

I married into Money. Seriously. That was the family name. They were English, from Southampton, the city that launched the Titanic. I noticed a stack of his mail and at first I thought it was a joke: Mr. Money.

Mr. Money was a penny-pinching fiscal neurotic, who had a lot of anxiety about ... money. He was always very concerned that everything be fifty/fifty, and so for nearly twenty years of marriage we had separate bank accounts.

I met Mr. Money at Monroe's Tavern in Galway City, on the west coast of Ireland. He played guitar in a blues band. I asked if I could get up and sing. The front man said "yes," Mr. Money said "no."

The front man won.

I was small, quiet, and unassuming, until I hit the stage. I stood in the front of that packed pub, tapped out the tempo to the band,

and sang "Wild Women Don't Have the Blues," by Ida Cox:

"I've got a disposition and a way of my own. When my man starts kicking, I let him find another home ..."

I tore it up. Brought down the house. Standing ovation. They never saw it coming, including Mr. Money. I walked off stage and straight out the door. It was a dramatic exit. Also, I was tired and wanted to get to bed. The next morning Mr. Money came looking for me. He wanted to start a new blues band. I wanted to sing Irish music, but I went with it: a gig's a gig. The Irish love the blues, and a pub owner picked the name: The Honorary Blues Band.

Mr. Money was very pretty—a delicate Mick Jagger in a grey leather jacket. We brought out the worst in each other, and fought from day one. One night we had a situation that required the morning after medication. He said he would pay for half. It had to be 50/50. The drug was nauseating, his stance infuriating. I flew into a rage and set the tone of our relationship.

We got pregnant later. It was a mutual, intentional accident. He wanted to be a father. I wanted to be a mother. We wanted to play music. We thought we'd make a go of it. Mr. Money and I were married in the last trimester. We split the cost of the license fifty/fifty. The Money in-laws came over. They referred to England as the mainland. They made my Irish roots shudder. I made their stiff upper lips quiver. I kept my name, Finnegan, and we all kept our distance.

Mr. Money and I moved to New York City and raised our baby. Our first neighborhood was Bay Ridge in Brooklyn where I waited tables at a diner. While Mr. Money lived off his separate savings, I saved receipts for household items to prove I was pulling my weight, fifty/fifty. We won a housing lottery, and moved to Chelsea. Our baby went to elementary school, middle school, and high school. Then our baby went to college, and the apartment was empty—just me and Mr. Money, living fifty/fifty. It turns out that two halves do not make a whole.

The divorce was uncontested. It cost $500. That was two hundred and fifty dollars each.

TRACY DOOLITTLE McNALLY

Tracy Doolittle McNally is the former executive director of Historic Huguenot Street in New Paltz, past oresident of the Greene County Chamber of Commerce in Catskill, and past vice president of the United Way for Ulster County. Prior to her career in the nonprofit world, Tracy worked in corporate advertising as a copywriter for an international forest products company. Tracy is currently pursuing her lifelong passions of genealogy, classical ballet, and storytelling.

THE "M" WORD

Tracy Doolittle McNally

At age thirty-nine, I relocated to live and work in the Hudson Valley. Although jobs were hard to come by, I managed to land one as director of marketing and public relations at Benedictine Hospital, a Catholic hospital in Kingston. This was a big change from my previous corporate world. I knew little about hospital management and less about the Catholic Church, other than the church had tried to murder my French Huguenot ancestors in the early 1600s.

Not long after I began working, a Benedictine Sister asked me to assemble a team of four—myself included—to represent the hospital in a trivia contest to benefit another nonprofit agency. I wanted to tell the dear Sister that I'd rather poke needles in my eyes than play trivia, but since I was the new hire, I thought better of it and started searching for other players. I deliberately didn't ask any doctors to participate because I wanted to have fun and drink with the nurses. Few were game to play, and after multiple strikeouts, a colleague suggested that I approach Dr. Richard McNally. "He knows everything" she said, "music, poetry, Shakespeare, beer making, sports—and he's very nice; not like a doctor at all."

Dr. McNally and I had never met before, but on my very first day at the hospital I'd phoned him for the answer to a serious yet very awkward question posed to me by a newspaper reporter during a contentious and controversial hospital merger: "How does a laboratory in a Catholic hospital obtain sperm for fertility testing if the church prohibits masturbation?" When I relayed the question to the doctor, I avoided using the "m" word and simply asked, "How do you get sperm?" Dr. McNally replied, "Ms. Doolittle, if your mother hasn't already explained that to you, I'm not sure I can help."

Dr. McNally remembered me when, a few months later, I phoned him again, and he consented to join my trivia team.

The week before the contest, I'd rented an antique black-sequined dress for an upcoming Halloween party at a haunted Hudson River mansion. Since I couldn't alter the dress's ample bust line, I bought a pair of those silicone breast forms that "increase your bust by two bra cup sizes." The night of the trivia contest, I decided in the parking lot to put the breast forms to the test—to actually wear them and see if they stayed put. Sitting in my car, I scanned the area to make sure no one could see me and slipped them into place. Then off I went with those jelly-like forms wiggling under my red business suit.

Dr. McNally bought me a drink, and the contest began. I contributed little of value to our team, but toward the end of the evening, the God of Trivia threw me a bone with the following question: "Who wrote the poem that begins "The fog comes on little cat feet?"" No one knew the answer, not even the Good Doctor. But I did. "Carl Sandburg" I said to the judges, ever so pleased with myself for clinching a bottle of wine for the team. I went on to explain to anyone willing to listen how, when I was twelve-years-old, I wrote an essay about the poem, poking fun of the poet's metaphor in Mr. Kaye's English class at Scarsdale Junior High. Twenty-seven years later, that essay really paid off.

Ten months later, after that fateful night of trivia, Richard and I were married on Nantucket Island, despite my misleading him with those silicone forms. And in case you're still wondering how the Catholic hospital obtained sperm specimens, it turned out there was a loophole. Although the medical laboratory was located *in* the hospital, it wasn't actually owned *by* the hospital per se, enabling the patients to "m" as much as they liked without fear of going blind.

CARI PATTISON

The Reverend **Cari Pattison** has served ten years as the associate minister at The Reformed Church of Bronxville, New York. In addition to ministry, Cari trained as a jazzercise, yoga, barre, and Pilates instructor, seeking to inspire people in body and spirit. Originally from Kansas City, Cari studied English and Art at Kalamazoo College in Michigan and earned her Masters of Divinity at Princeton Theological Seminary in New Jersey. She previously taught eighth-grade English in Missouri, and served a variety of churches and hospitals in Kansas, Kenya, and New Jersey. Cari has blogged for the *Huffington Post*, illustrated the children's book *ABC: Sing with Me*, and is a 2015 recipient of the Kathryn Gurfein Fellowship at The Writing Institute of Sarah Lawrence College.

DEARLY BELOVED

Cari Pattison

I get invited to a lot of weddings. Not for my wide circle of friends nor my charm as a guest, and not for my connections to yacht clubs or my fashion sense—unless you're into black wool.

I go to so many weddings because I officiate them. As an ordained minister, I show the groom how to place the ring on his bride without jamming her finger, and store tissues in my folder for unexpected tears during the vows. I crafted a "Midsummer Night's Dream" wedding for one couple. For another, I agreed to let them include in their ceremony: "I love being naughty with you." I'm a sucker for a good love story.

But the minister role can be a delicate one. I've sat across from two twenty-somethings and watched the girl's face fall when her fiancé said he didn't believe in marriage. I advised them to perhaps postpone the wedding. The bride called the next day to fire me so they could find an officiant who would be "more supportive."

One summer, a couple rented our sanctuary for their large-scale wedding and all went well until their church hierarchy told them female pastors were not allowed. "That's inconvenient," I said, "since the male clergy are away, and at least one of us has to co-officiate." The bride consulted their bishop, and called to say, "Turns out you can't do any minister parts, but you've been granted special permission to light the unity candle."

Unity …is not my specialty. I officiated my first-ever wedding the same week I told my husband I wanted to separate. In a cruel bit of irony, my nickname for him was "Dearly Beloved," or "Dearly" for short.

After my marriage ended, I flew out to Ohio to officiate my brother George's wedding. Some of my relatives had been silent since my divorce, and I pictured standing before disapproving family members who prided themselves on "making marriage work." When I shared my fears, my mom said, "You don't have to officiate."

But memories of George flashed through my mind: the three-year-old circling the basement in a big wheel, the six-year-old shooting hoops in the driveway, the ten-year-old jumping off the diving board—always saying, "Did you see that, Cari? How 'bout me? The Number One! How 'bout me? The MVP!" I babysat him, played board games with him, and built bed tents with him. No one but me would pronounce him somebody's husband.

At the hotel in Columbus, I went outside to review my notes. My dad's friend Dave stepped out for a cigarette. "Can I have one?" I said. Knowing I don't smoke, he laughed, "How's it going, Preacher?" A former Air Force technician with thick white hair, Dave had married my mom's friend after she caught his eye wearing leopard-print pants. It was his third marriage.

I confessed my doubts: "I don't exactly feel like the love-and-marriage guru right now." Dave looked me square in the eye and said, "You've got this."

An hour later at the chapel, there was George, standing in front of me in gray suit and green-and-navy-striped tie, shifting his weight from left to right. The kid brother I remembered was now a man I loved so fiercely it was all I could do to keep the tears behind my eyes from spilling out into the pews.

And there behind that wooden podium, I let go my tale of woe, my fears of what anyone thought because there was a love story to tell, and I got to be the one to tell it—to bless and pray and endorse and point to the source of all love—the One who's there, even when the story changes.

I looked out and took a deep breath.

"Dearly Beloved ... " I began.

I smiled at my brother, the MVP, and knew right then, I was right where I needed to be.

SHEILA COLLINS

Sheila D. Collins is Professor Emerita of Political Science at William Paterson University where she headed its graduate program in Public Policy and International Affairs. She is the author and/ or editor of six books on American politics, public policy, social movements and religion, two poetry chapbooks and numerous book chapters and articles. Her blogs have appeared on *Huffington Post, Truthout, New Politics, Oxford University Press* and *Religion Dispatches*. She is currently working on a biography of a social activist and, now that she is retired, is delighted to have time to take a memoir writing class at Sarah Lawrence College and to finish work that she began years ago.

ROYAL WEDDING

Sheila Collins

In the 1940s, Toronto, where I spent my early years, was still very much a part of the British Commonwealth in culture and tradition. The descendants of the Empire's riff-raff seemed to cling to the standard of empire long after it had faded. It was the Royals who claimed our deepest affections and the Union Jack flew at our public occasions. I always thought my grandma was related to the House of Windsor, for she looked just like the Queen Mother. I could picture Grandma's benign head and waving hand poking out of the gilded, horse-drawn carriages that carried the Royal Family through the glossy pages of *McCall's*, and the sumptuous descriptions of yet another Royal wedding or coronation.

As a child, my favorite pastime was pouring over grandma's wedding memorabilia. According to the *Toronto Star*, grandma's wedding was "one of the prettiest of the season, the bride handsomely gowned in ivory directoire satin, trimmed with pearls and lace. She wore a veil caught with orange blossoms and carried a large shower bouquet of lilies of the valley and white roses."

At the far end of grandma's parlor stood a brick fireplace, whose mantel formed the backdrop for the official wedding pictures of the four Johnston girls, taken at two-year intervals. Each daughter is dressed in grandma's own directoire satin gown. By this time, its high neck had been cut off and the neckline scraped into a shallow scoop in keeping with changing fashions. Although the faces changed, the photos are identical, down to the right arm through that of the new husband's, the bridesmaids in long taffeta gowns with matching hats and nosegays.

I'm in one of those wedding pictures, a beaming, round-faced flower girl of eight, with a shiny, turned-up nose, blonde hair wound in tight Shirley Temple ringlets, holding a basket of daisies. It was at my favorite Aunt Lois' wedding, the one who had made me see fairies and was able to make coins disappear and reappear in my ear. My Uncle Chas, her high school sweetheart, is next to her, a skinny, long-nosed, sallow-faced lad sprouting a large pompadour. I can still remember the thrill of being fitted for that pale green taffeta gown with the delicate pink lace inset in the bodice and receiving a real sterling silver bracelet as a present from the bride. With awestruck trepidation I marched down that long central aisle of High Park United Church, no longer banished from the grown-ups' service to some subterranean Sunday school room, but here, marching at the center of this splendid Royal wedding!

This was going to be the wedding I would have when I was

grown up. Like my mother and aunts before me, I would wear grandma's gown and be surrounded with bridesmaids in identical taffeta dresses.

But by the time my own wedding arrived, Grandma's gown was yellow and moth-eaten. My husband-to-be was so scared of marriage—having cancelled a wedding years earlier—and spent years in therapy trying to get over his guilt and fear of intimacy that he gave me three days to prepare—while he ran off to an island off the coast of Maine without a telephone so he wouldn't be tempted to back out. I quickly called my childhood friend, Patty, to ask if she would be my bridesmaid and rushed down to Lerner's to buy a white cocktail dress. Three days later, my wedding pictures were taken by my stepfather (whom my mother was in the process of discarding) with a brownie camera and a weak flash. The minister, picked too quickly for the occasion, read that awful passage from Scripture about wives having to be obedient to their husbands. In the barely visible light of the East Harlem church, the men all look like Mafia dons and all you can see of me are my bright pink rabbit eyes.

AVIVA NAJMAN

Aviva Najman received a BFA in fine art from Queens College and studied with the artists Mercedes Matter and Rosemary Back in an intensive two-year drawing and painting program at the historic New York Studio School. Aviva went on to earn an MA in Modern and Contemporary Art History from Christie's, and worked at the Zach Feuer Gallery in Chelsea. Aviva continues to paint and draw, and teach art in her home in Chestnut Ridge, New York. Recently, Aviva has taken writing courses at Sarah Lawrence College where she has studied with the humorist Dan Zevin, the insightful Marian Thurm, and the venerable *El Jefe*, Steven Lewis. All this time, Aviva has devoted the bulk of her energy to raising four intelligent and caring children. This is her masterpiece, still in progress.

YOU COULD SLEEP IN A CAR

Aviva Najman

You could sleep in a car. What you do is park it in the lot of the Days Inn, the one behind the Target next to the thruway. If it's raining and dark outside, that's even better because who would come out and check the cars in the rain? The pillow that props you up because the seat adjuster is broken is really all you need to make a nice sleeping situation for yourself. Also, lucky for you, this is a Mercedes with soft leather seats.

Now, try to remember if the windows are tinted, because that would be lucky too. The worst thing would be if a family, drowsy and desperate, parks right next to you and as the dad carries the toddler out of her carseat, she picks her head up from his shoulder and stares into the window of your car and sees a lump on the seat, and she stares and points to ask daddy "what's that?" So the father will need to answer or else the baby will fixate and then won't go back to sleep and for God's sake it's three o'clock in the morning.

So he glances, but then the image coalesces, and this time he sees that it's not a jumble of clothes but a lady, with her head on a gray cushion, and her hand, glowing white, peeking out from the pile of jacket and hair and pillow. He might knock on the window, "Hey are you okay?" You will awaken immediately and rearrange your features, you are calm as the sea, "Yes, everything is fine." You send out normalcy vibes that soothe the man.

You are tired, the rain is noisy, the car is chilly, and you are tired. So you decide that the windows are tinted. You throw the pillow into the back seat, and climb over the center cubby barely closed over crumpled receipts and chewing gum packets. He buys those packets by the box because he has an oral fixation, and if he is not constantly chewing gum, he will chew food, and not vegetables either. Your phone is on silent because his texting is disturbing you. It is a great idea to put the phone on silent until the sun comes up and you are not so tired.

You put the pillow up against the door handle, and you pull your rain jacket over you face because your pale skin is a beacon in the night and as carefully explained above, you do not need anyone knocking and disturbing your rest. By this time, you have about ten texts from him but it's fine, since you have the phone on silent. But you worry because what if he is so worried that he dials 911, and then he gives them your jacket or headband to smell and then they find you, how embarrassing. Then, for sure, everyone will know that you are insane. So you text back something neutral like, I am fine, just want to sleep. Call you later! This does not calm him. The texts are coming fast, ?where are you, where are you?"

When you were eighteen, you were sure that the future was in a loft somewhere in Gowanus, living and sleeping in a studio that smelled like paint. The bathroom down the hall would be for boys and girls and everyone would be poor and have the radio on all the time. You would be a bit of a bum, which is okay because you don't need to shower that much and you are fine with one meal a day. What you ended up with instead was a night in a car behind the Days Inn, your face smashed into a couch cushion, clutching your phone so close to your mouth that the screen is damp, reading his texts, and waiting impatiently for the next one to appear.

JULIE TRELSTAD

Julie Trelstad is the Director of Julie Ink Creative Author Consulting, an agency specializing in helping authors grow their online presence. An expert in book publishing, Julie has spent two decades on the frontlines of the digital publishing frontier. For most of her career, Julie was an acquisitions editor for homebuilding, architecture, and construction books working at various publishers including Reader's Digest, The Taunton Press, and John Wiley & Sons. She's best known for acquiring the book *The Not So Big House* by Sarah Susanka. Before founding Julie Ink, Julie spent several years at Writers House, a literary agency where she managed the agency's digital publishing program. When she's not dancing or helping authors, Julie is currently finishing her first novel.

THE SALSA LESSON

Julie Trelstad

Five years ago, I took a salsa lesson on a whim. I tripped over my feet trying to do the basic step. But I liked the teacher and I had always wanted to learn how to dance, so I came back the next week, and then every week thereafter for more than a year. The class was Latin Shines, and the best part—I didn't need a partner. That was important because my husband refused to dance.

That fact made me sad. After twenty years of marriage, a lot of things made me angry, too. Our twin daughters had just left home for college, and I wanted to try new things. But he just wanted to stay home. I got to a point where I was prepared to walk out on my marriage if I was going to spend the rest of my life with a man who refused to dance.

For his birthday, I gave my husband a pair of dance shoes and six months to figure it out.

We started couple's therapy and private salsa lessons at the same time. In therapy, we traced the patterns that we'd worn into the floor of our marriage, the ones we'd repeated so many times that we had come in danger of falling through. In salsa lessons, we learned new patterns.

"One little detail," says our instructor Carlos as he walks me back to the middle of the dance studio. He poses my fingers—pinky up, middle fingers slightly dipped, the delicate inside of my elbow exposed. I count. There are ten little details.

Carlos leaves me to practice alone. Fluttering with self-consciousness, I move my arm in and out like a baby bird—shoulder, elbow, wrist, fingers—while Carlos corrects my husband Graham's hand signals and shows him how to lead.

Graham looks perplexed. "I can't always get her to do what I want her to do. Sometimes she just stands there."

Carlos smiles. "If we pull too hard, they spin too soon. Too soft, they make things up."

Graham listens, nods. A wide grin breaks his face. "Who's in control? I am!"

In the language of the dance studio, as in many other places, the men are "we," and women are "they." In the opposing sides of salsa, I seem to be on the wrong one. I want to be the one to lead. Why can't I spin when I want to?

Carlos can see that we're getting tired. He leads us over to the stereo cabinet and offers us a sip of cafecito. It's not even nine o'clock. As we caffeinate, shake off our morning fog, Carlos lectures us that relaxing is the most important little detail.

"Grab my arm." Like a boy on a playground showing his muscles, he tenses so hard that moving it is like lifting a heavy weight.

"That's what you're doing to him," he says to me. "Relax."

"Yes!" says Graham as if letting go were something I could easily do in a situation involving three-inch heels and ever-more-complicated choreography.

My heels snap on the wood as we return for another round. Graham is noiseless in his plain black Capezios.

In the first months of our lessons, I refused to look Graham in the eye. I blamed it on trying to get my feet to do the foreign steps, but mostly I wanted to run away as much as I wanted to learn to dance.

Our therapist taught us that there are three of us in the relationship—me, Graham, and the couple.

Our couple makes the dance. In the dance, we're not equals, we're both halves. He leads. I follow. Our steps fall into sync. I'm learning to be okay with that. Even if it contradicts my sense of self as a modern woman.

Graham spins me. I feel weightless. Carlos stops us. "One more little detail."

STEVEN LEWIS

Steven Lewis, Literary Ombudsman for Read650, is a columnist at *Talking Writing*, and a member of the Sarah Lawrence College Writing Institute faculty. A longtime freelancer, his work has been published in *The New York Times*, *The Washington Post*, *Christian Science Monitor*, the *Los Angeles Times*, *Ploughshares*, *Spirituality & Health* and others. Recent novels include *Take This*, *Loving Violet*, and *A Hard Rain*, all from Codhill Press, and Finishing Line Press published Steve's poetry chapbook, *If I Die Before You Wake*. His backlist includes *Zen and the Art of Fatherhood*, *The ABCs of Real Family Values*, *The Complete Guide for the Anxious Groom*, and *Fear and Loathing of Boca Raton (a Hippie's Guide to the New Sixties)*. He divides his time between his writing space in New Paltz, New York and Hatteras Island, North Carolina.

SOMETHING IN THE WAY SHE MOVES

Steven Lewis

Standing alone in the Rathskellar, tray in her hands, a vision in a red University of Wisconsin sweatshirt, red plaid slacks, and red Keds. She was drop-dead gorgeous: sculpted face, long straight hair, the sway of her back creating an instant yearning in the hollow of my throat.

She was obviously leaving, but I was too shy, too thick-tongued to approach such a stunning creature.

Not my new roommate. A worldly hipster from Darien, Connecticut, he already knew the retching glories of peyote while I was still finding God through tiny straws, sipping 7 and 7s. Roommate abandoned me before I had a chance to tuck in my new madras shirt.

So it goes. And so it went over the next three years, as she and roommate did the undergraduate make-up-break-up-dosey-doe dozens of times. Meanwhile, I was slowly gaining the kind of clarity about relationships that only good weed—and a girlfriend with ulcerative colitis whose MD father specialized in ulcerative colitis—can bring.

Late one evening, perhaps early morning—reeling down the middle of Langdon Street in a state of high clarity, I declared to one and all that I would never get married—such a boojie convention!—and that I would never ever bring an innocent child into this corrupt world.

I would live life as a hermit poet in Nova Scotia.

A month later, Patti and the roommate had their final final final breakup—and girlfriend had flushed me out of her life. Thus, in mutual commiseration, on December 10, 1967, Patti Henderson and I stumbled into our first date.

I know the exact day because I had scored two tickets for girlfriend and me to see the great Otis Redding at the Dane County Arena—and that night his plane crashed into the frozen waters of Lake Monona.

It was an inauspicious beginning to a relationship, for sure, but a few mournful hours and one lusciously sad goodnight kiss later, I officially abandoned all self-righteous declarations about love and marriage.

And through the coming spring, I asked and I asked and maybe I begged until she agreed … and finally in August we tied the knot in steamy New Orleans. A month later, a full fifteen minutes after our first adult conversation about the necessity of waiting to have children, we were naked and making a baby.

Forty-eight years later, I'm still slack-jawed at the implications of all that. Dumbfounded as I occasionally speculate on how my life would have been different had roommate and I arrived at the Rathskellar thirty seconds later. Patti would have been gone—and the likelihood of ever seeing her again on a campus with 40,000 students was beyond beyond unlikely.

I never would have shared a single moment with a girl, then a woman, to whom I am drawn every moment of my life in vast unspeakable ways. And maybe more confounding, our children would not exist! Seven of them.

Nor the sixteen grandchildren. It boggles the mind.

Some people would explain our unlikely meeting and long life together as a "meant to be." Very sweet, but you'd have to be high on crack to believe that kind of nonsense in this vast incomprehensible universe where divorce, insanity, drug addiction, cancer, murder, and mayhem of all kinds would also have to be considered "meant to be"s.

After forty-eight years, though, through all the better and worse, through the thin and the thickening, through this glass darkly, I've learned enough to leave the unanswerable questions alone and just be humbled by the perfectly precarious nature of our unlikely lives together.

I am grateful, when I'm not being an ingrate, for the morsels of grace we've shared with each other, for the twenty-three people whose lives were made livable by one chance meeting, for this hollow in my throat that never goes away.

EDWARD McCANN

Edward McCann is an award winning writer/producer and the founder and editor of *Read650*, celebrating the spoken word with live events in New York City and throughout the tri-state area. A long-time contributing editor to *Country Living*, his features and essays have been published in many literary journals, anthologies, and national magazines, including *Better Homes & Gardens, Good Housekeeping, The Irish Echo, The Sun,* and others. His essay, "Pregnant Again," was selected for the anthology, *Listen To Your Mother,* published by Penguin, and he's recently completed a memoir about the search for his missing nephew. He lives and writes in a pastoral spot about eighty miles north of New York City and is at work on a collection of essays about life in the Hudson Valley.

TWO GROOMS

Edward McCann

"I don't want a cake with two grooms on top," Richard said.

"And we're not dressing up like Tom Wolfe," I added.

"Let's just get married and have a party sometime this summer," Richard said.

"And we won't even call it a wedding," I replied.

Mimi, the marriage clerk at Kingston City Hall, beamed, congratulating us with hugs and tiny bag of M&M's. With our license valid for sixty days, we consulted our schedules and added the event as if it were any other appointment—like a trip to the DMV to renew a vehicle registration.

Richard and I had shared a business and a home for over fifteen years. We'd both been married before—to women—and had no desire to stand on a receiving line, to dance a first dance, to make or listen to a speech. We have supportive friends, family—even clients, and we're as committed to one another as any two people can possibly be. Over the years we've already shared "better and worse," supporting each other through loss, grief, and illness, including a summer of radiation therapy. Richard, joking, asked me to marry him long before—a moment I'll never forget—but we'd never expected legal marriage to become a possibility in our lifetimes.

Years earlier, our attorney drafted some documents to enable us to protect each other's interests—wills and powers of attorney and some other papers, just in case. We weren't sure we needed to get married, but something stirred within me the summer New York made gay marriage legal, when I saw images of the jubilant gay couples who rushed to be married at midnight, double brides and double grooms, mature couples like Richard and me—partners who'd been together for years, thrilled, finally, to have their commitment codified by the state.

Despite those "just in case" papers I carried from state to state in my briefcase, I knew that, in an emergency, it would only take one unenlightened nurse to place a wall between Richard and me, and chilling stories of gay couples in crisis loomed large: A car accident; the sudden reappearance of an estranged family member assuming the mantle of "next of kin," the "long-term companion" shut out, refused entry, refused access, refused information.

This simply doesn't happen to married people. In a "straight" crisis, "That's my wife in there" suffices, a few simple words that grant one person admission to his rightful place beside another, without presenting documents or even a wedding ring. Richard and I simply wanted that same protection, and once we made the decision, we reached for our calendars.

"It should be a Tuesday or a Thursday," Richard said, "so it doesn't conflict with our gym schedule."

"Right," I said, surveying the weeks ahead. "And afterwards we'll have lunch or dinner someplace."

We asked two close friends to be our witnesses, and booked a lunch table at The Mohonk Mountain House, a historic, Victorian, mountain-top hotel in New Paltz. Focused then on deadlines, it wasn't until our wedding day was upon us that I realized how very different this was from the other events filling the schedule; it was nothing at all like a trip to the DMV, or a chiropractor appointment. Richard and I were finally, actually, going to marry, and it felt like a very big deal.

At Ulster County Family Court, we stood in Judge Tony's office, between a desk and sofa. I had butterflies.

"I'm going to use any magic words to marry you," Tony said. "You just have to say, out loud, in front of me, that you wish to marry each other. If you've prepared something, you can say anything else you like."

I took Richard's hands, looked him square in the eye, and the two of us made promises.

I could see forever from where I stood. And I already knew that forever wouldn't be long enough.

ACKNOWLEDGMENTS

In addition to the contributors to this volume, we thank Patricia Dunn and The Writing Institute at Sarah Lawrence College for inviting us to produce this event on their stage. The Writing Institute helps writers in all genres progress and grow in their craft, and welcomes them all into a very supportive community.

SarahLawrence.edu

We thank Nancy Manocherian's the cell, which supported 650 at its inception. A twenty-first century salon in the heart of New York City, their mission is to support the arts and incubate new works, and the cell made its beautiful performance space available to 650 as we were finding our way. The cell: To mine the mind, pierce the heart, and awaken the soul.

TheCellTheatre.org

Artists Without Walls was created to inspire, uplift, and unite people and communities of diverse cultures through the pursuit of artistic achievement, and has supported and encouraged 650 from its beginnings. Artists Without Walls: No Limits. No Walls. No Boundaries.

ArtistsWithoutWalls.com

READ650.COM

INFO @READ650.COM
FACEBOOK.COM/READ650